THIS JOURNAL IS TO HELP YOU EASE YOUR MIND OF THE NEGATIVE CONCEPTS OF LIFE EVERYDAY PETTY MENTAL STRUGGLES

By truly being honest with yourself, you are putting yourself in the first step to heal and be open to change ....
Your everyday mental life struggles would not weigh you down so heavy.

Disclaimer

These are steps to better yourself in a positive way, no one is going to like it who was toxic to you. They may say you can't do it or you think you better than whoever. You CAN do it. YOU CAN achieve mental peace and a better life. The better friends , Man, & New Family will come. You just have to believe in yourself & PUT IN THE WORK TO STAND ON <u>YOUR OWN</u> TWO FEET. The people who value you will accept your positive growth as the next stage in your life. You can take one step or all steps to help you grow mentally, but know it's up to you. You got this!!!

Everyday Life Struggles
The Basics

1. Work Thoughts

2. Home Mindfulness

3. Family & Friends Boundaries

4. Self Care

You are the creator of your life. Only you can make a positive change

Work Thoughts

Are you happy at your job?

1 We all know you have to work to make money, but it is possible to be happy with what you're doing? It's easier said than done to up and get a dream job, but you can prepare your mindset now to be able to transition into something better.

Work Thoughts

If you're happy with your job:
What ways you can become better in your work field?

What ways you can move up in management?

If you are not happy with your job:
What job would you like to go towards?

What requirements do you need to gain or already have to obtain the new job?

What are your goals with the new job?

Either decision you make put your best foot forward to reach your highest good especially with your finances.

Work Thoughts

Advice

Wake up early enough to be at least 5 to 10 minutes early for work. This is so you can get into a better mindset already at work on time then running late rushing to work. We want to keep our money long and mind at peace. Rushing due to constantly hitting that snooze button is not it.

Bring lunch from home. Buying food is good at times, but everyday it is not. Use that money for other things. Yes you may have the money to do so, but the gas used to get there, money spent, the type of quick food and time spent to eat it is a lot on a lunch break. Eliminate a lot of rushing on lunch breaks. We trying to ease our mind and pockets.

Work Thoughts

Advice

Do not overindulge with your coworkers about your personal business. I know we are around these people longer than our families, but your job should be separate from your personal life. Keep the conversations on the surface.

My Notes _____ Date : _____

My Notes

Date:

My Notes _____   Date: _____

My Notes _____ Date : _____

My Notes _____   Date: _____

My Notes

Date:

My Notes _____ Date : _____

My Notes

Date :

My Notes _____ Date : _____

My Notes

Date:

My Notes _____   Date : _____

Home Mindfulness 2

How does your living space / car look?

As busy as life gets we have to be mindful in how we navigate in the world around us. Clutter and disorganization causes us not to be focus on the simple things in life which turn into bigger things later on. Mess equals stress. Let's ease your mind, by tackling things you keep putting off so there can be no mental obstacles to focus on something new for your positive growth.

Home Mindfulness

WHAT AREAS IN YOUR LIFE NEEDS THE MOST ATTENTION IN REGARDS TO DECLUTTERING?

WHAT WAYS ARE YOU ABLE TO DECLUTTER YOUR SPACE?

WHAT STEPS WILL YOU TAKE TO STAY CONSISTENT IN MAINTAINING A DECLUTTERED SPACE

IN WHAT OTHER AREAS IN YOUR LIFE CAN YOU DECLUTTER? PEOPLE, PLACES, & THINGS

If it's too Mentally stressful and do not benefit your growth in your present moment & you Honestly know the same pattern will be in the near future declutter (let go) Of that person / people, places, & things (Drugs, financial irresponsibility, unhealthy diet habits, negative mindset towards others & self).

Focus on you in a healthy way

Home Mindfulness
Advice

Even though it's hard to find the time to do the basic things in life we have to make time to ease our mind. By taking the first step to organizing your life it will become a habit with consistency.

You don't have to be a neat freak but being more aware of how you let things go into clutter and stop it in its tracks can free up mental space for "new" Things.

Instead of leaving laundry laying around fold them and put them away

Home Mindfulness
Advice

Take 30 minutes before you go to bed to clean your space. Waking up to a better visual of your surroundings can put you in a calmer mood.

Stop bad habits that you know are not good for you.
 (Drugs, financial irresponsibility, unhealthy diet habits, negative mindset towards others & self).

Let those people, places & things go that do not have a positive impact on your present. You future will be great, but by decluttering the negative things that is holding you back & staying consistent on bringing positive things into your life; you will get there sooner.

My Notes _____ Date: _____

My Notes _____ Date: _____

My Notes _____ Date: _____

My Notes _____ Date: _____

My Notes

Date :

My Notes _____ Date : _____

My Notes   Date :

My Notes _____   Date : _____

My Notes _____   Date: _____

My Notes _____ Date : _____

My Notes _____ Date : _____

Family & Friends boundaries 2

Learn to love from a distance & walk away unapologetically

We know family is a touchy subject to cross, but sometimes that can be a big part of our mental chaos. It can take time, but you can heal from the childhood traumas and / or present negativity. It's ok to move on from negative family members and live YOUR life as YOU see fit. They lived theirs the way they thought was best, but what is best for you ONLY YOU can choose that by living in your true authenticity.

Friends have a way of being our mini families when we are being our true self outside of the family we deal with. Friends often times see our more personal ups and downs. This is why a toxic friend stays around longer than they should. No matter how much history you have with a person:

Family & Friends boundaries 2

Learn to love from a distance & walk away unapologetically

Are they constantly talking behind you back & you keep finding out?
Are you constantly noticing the slick hate towards you in their "Oh I'm just playing" Jokes towards you or towards people about you.
Are you constantly seeing a copy cat in them for stealing your style, talk, lifestyle?

It is sooo much more to go off of, but you get my drift on toxic friends. If these are people in your circle no matter the history it's time to grow from that. Always remember they will bring you the gossip of other people drama & spill yours too. There is no time for these type of friends. No one is perfect, but toxic should not be normal in your life.

Family & Friends boundaries

These questions are to be answered for family on one paper and friends on another paper. Be honest with yourself in your responses.

In what ways are your family/ friend hurting your feelings?

When you accomplished the smallest things/big things what are your family / friend initial reaction towards it? Are they happy or dismiss the subject?

Do you show up more (be there for) for your family / friend more then they do for you?

In what ways will you choose yourself to be in a better positive mindset when dealing with the family/ friend?

How will you stay consistent in noticing the patterns of a toxic family / friend and removing yourself from the situation?

Family & Friends Boundaries

Advice

If you have constantly lended out money and that Family/Friend have not paid you back then try to ask for more money or got mad if you didn't give more money let them go and keep your money. People will misuse your kindness to their advantage.

When you start growing you let go a lot of old ways and mindset those toxic families/friends can be apart of that letting go. Your peace and your growth in a positive way means sooo much more. When setting boundaries with the words "NO" can make a lot of people mad, but why are they mad? You cut off the toxic way they used you and that's not healthy for your mental and money.

If you were surrounded by people who were toxic and you cut them out of your life it's ok. It may seem lonely at first, but you regain your power back. True friends will come that are more healthier to your growth, because you learned the lessons of self worth.

My Notes _____ Date: _____

My Notes _____ Date : _____

My Notes _____ Date: _____

My Notes _____ Date: _____

My Notes _____ Date: _____

My Notes

Date:

My Notes _____ Date : ____

My Notes _____ Date : _____

My Notes _____ Date: _____

My Notes _____   Date : _____

My Notes _____ Date: _____

Self Care

Follow Your Intuition

4 Mainstream media shadows self care as spas, shopping sprees, beauty maintenance etc. This is part of it to make you feel and look beautiful, but it is also so much more. Self Care is also in making sure your mind, body, spirituality (whatever you believe in or not believe in) is balance. To start that journey of Self Care balance the first step is easing the everyday struggles of negativity in your life. You are doing that by tackling your:

Work Thoughts
Home Mindfulness
Family & Friends Boundaries
For Your Mental Self Care Towards Growth for YOUR Future.

Self Care

How do you feel about coming to your conclusion on tackling your work thoughts?

How do you feel about coming to your conclusion on tackling your home mindfulness?

How do you feel about coming to your conclusion on tackling your family & friends boundaries?

These steps will change your life for a positive path towards your growth. You have chosen to stand firm with your self worth. What ways will you handle the loneliness and backlash? (Know that this is for your growth)

Self Care
ADVICE

Being Consistent is hard when you make excuses why you can't do things to help you in your positive growth. Stop making excuses And implement ways to enhance yourSelf for YOUR highest good.

Excercise to build energy to help carry you on this new journey. Working out 3 to 5 days a week consistently will not only transform your body to be even more gorgeous, but also strengthen your mind with clarity.

Follow YOUR Intuition: You know when you need to do things (anything & any situation) trust yourself.

My Notes _____ Date : _____

My Notes _____ Date : _____

My Notes _____ Date: _____

My Notes _____   Date: _____

My Notes _____ Date : _____

My Notes _____ Date :

My Notes _____   Date : _____

My Notes _____ Date: _____

My Notes _____ Date : _____

My Notes _____ Date : _____

My Notes _____ Date: _____

My Notes _____ Date : _____

My Notes _____ Date: _____

My Notes   Date :

My Notes _____ Date: _____

My Notes _____   Date: _____

My Notes _____ Date : _____

My Notes _____ Date: _____

My Notes _____ Date : _____

www.ingramcontent.com/pod-product-compliance
Lightning Source LLC
Chambersburg PA
CBHW051258110526
44589CB00025B/2871